MW01613375

"But they that wait upon the LORD shall renew their strength; they shall mount up with wings as eagles; they shall run, and not be weary; and they shall walk, and not faint."

Isaiah 40:31

Renewed Strength

Renewed Strength, now in its second printing, is a compilation of printed sermons by Pastor James C. Johnson which all focus on pursuing heaven-sent strength. Christians, we are not alone in our need for divine strength; for we share this necessity with Bible characters as well as Christians throughout the ages. This content is produced by Strength for Life which is a ministry of NorthStone Baptist Church in Pensacola, Florida. The SFL team, led by Pastor Johnson, is passionate about getting Biblical principles into the hands and hearts of people all around the world.

SFL agrees with John Jay, our country's first Supreme Court Justice, when he said, "The Bible is the best of all books, for it is the Word of God and teaches us the way to be happy in this world and in the next. Continue therefore to read it and to regulate your life by its precepts."

Further, SFL believes that the ONLY way to have "good success" is to meditate on the Word of God and "observe to do according to all that is written therein." (Joshua 1:8)

For more SFL visit, www.strengthforlife.church.

Renewed Strength

Foreword

I am pleased to recommend *Renewed Strength* to anyone seeking encouragement in life's journey. It's no secret that new and mounting pressures in society at large have challenged even the most stoic of men and women. In *Renewed Strength*, Pastor Johnson looks to the Scriptures for the timeless truths necessary to face life's new challenges with courage and stamina. By directing us anew to the Lord, and by explaining our obligation to wait upon Him in trust and confidence, *Renewed Strength* brings us to the Source of genuine confidence.

Pastor Johnson does not approach life with rose-colored glasses, nor does he promote a "positive thinking" approach. Rather, he acknowledges the challenges of life and gives practical and biblical solutions to overcoming the challenges we face with strength and dignity. *Renewed Strength* teaches us how to rise above the clouds of life, how to live perennially in the celestial sunshine of God's grace.

Pastor Johnson's message could not be more timely, nor his prescriptions more timeless. May the people of God "mount up with wings as eagles" to face the challenges of our generation.

Pastor Marc G. Monte

Avon, Indiana

Introduction

"But they that wait upon the LORD shall renew their strength; they shall mount up with wings as eagles; they shall run, and not be weary; and they shall walk, and not faint." ~ Isaiah 40:31

This verse is one of the most inspirational and beautiful verses in all of Scripture. For the sake of understanding Isaiah 40:31 in its context, and for the sake of applying these timeless truths to our daily lives, we will break this verse down into four sections. We will consider the Lord, the Wait, the Strength, and the Activity of Isaiah 40:31.

the Lord

Possibly, when we read Isaiah 40:31, we are immediately drawn to the promise of renewed strength. At times, we all feel weak and overwhelmed by life's circumstances, and the offer of renewed strength sounds both intriguing and refreshing. To me, this verse has its appeal in the description of flying effortlessly, running tirelessly, and walking energetically. However, before any of the benefits of this verse can be realized, Isaiah wants the reader to consider the LORD of Isaiah 40. "They that wait upon the LORD shall…."

Before we can receive the promise described in the verse, Isaiah wants us to reflect on the Provider of that promise. After all, the Jewish people of Isaiah's day had concluded that the Lord had stopped providing for them. Their complaint about the Lord is briefly explained in Isaiah 40:27.

"Why sayest thou, O Jacob, and speakest, O Israel, My way is hid from the LORD, and my judgment is passed over from my God?"

They felt like the Lord wasn't watching over them anymore, as if they were hidden from Him. They were saying that the Lord disregarded or "passed over" their cause.

Essentially, they felt abandoned by the Lord. Their complaint was based on the specific circumstance of Sennacherib's invading Israel. The Assyrian king had laid siege on Jerusalem and desecrated the Temple. Imagine being a Jewish person in that situation. It's reasonable to think that they felt like they were free-falling into uncertainty. Doubts, fears, and anxieties were flooding their minds. Isaiah comforts them by not just describing the potential for renewed strength, but more importantly, he endeavors to realign their focus on the character of the Lord. They were allowing the chaos of their situation to skew their view of God, and as a result, Isaiah spends most of Isaiah 40 realigning their view of God by describing His true character. Isaiah calls to this weak and struggling people, "Behold your God." (Isaiah 40:9)

Regularly ruminating on the Bible's many accounts of the character of the Lord is a spiritually healthy thing to do, especially when we're experiencing times of uncertainty and trial.

It's important for believers to love God, not just for what He can do for us, but also for who He is. Let us together be reminded of who "the LORD" of Isaiah 40:31 truly is. As I read through Isaiah 40, I see twelve characteristics of the Lord.

1) The Lord is Holy (Isaiah 40:2)

"…She [Jerusalem] hath received of the LORD's hand double for all her sins."

Notice God's attention to Judah's sins. God must judge sin because His holiness demands it, but God is set apart from sin; there is no sin in Him. God is pure. In our culture, purity is often rightly equated with value. Pure gold or a pure diamond is more valuable than fool's gold or a tainted diamond.

The Lord we need in times of uncertainty is not encumbered with the sinful temptations and vices of this world. He is set apart from sin; and therefore, He can be trusted in our times of trial. We ought to value the pure holiness of the Lord because it means that He is set apart from the muck and mire of this sinful world.

Isaiah 6 describes Him as "Holy, holy, holy, is the LORD of hosts…." His holiness is triune. He is Holy God the Father, Holy God the Son, and Holy God the Holy Ghost. Behold your God in His holiness!

2) The Lord is Willful (Isaiah 40:4)

"Every valley shall be exalted, and every mountain and hill shall be made low: and the crooked shall be made straight, and the rough places plain."

The Lord can make a valley into a mountain, and He can turn a mountain into a valley. If He wills it, He can make the crooked straight and the rough places plain. God can do anything He wants. Your situation may seem like an insurmountable mountain or a scary, deep valley, yet if He wills, He can completely reverse your situation. Behold your God in the power of His willfulness!

3) The Lord is Glorious (Isaiah 40:5)

"And the glory of the LORD shall be revealed."

His glory is revealed specifically in the willful acts described in verse 4. Notice that each of those acts references His creation. His glory is clearly seen in His power over creation. He is the Creator of heaven and earth and He is our Creator. He created you! (Isaiah 40:26, 28) Marvel at the glorious abilities of the Lord. Behold your God in His glory!

4) The Lord is Superior (Isaiah 40:6,7)

"All flesh is grass, and all the goodliness thereof is as the flower of the field. The grass withereth, the flower fadeth: because the spirit of the LORD bloweth upon it: surely the people is grass."

Before we can receive the renewed strength of Isaiah 40:31, Isaiah puts the reader in his place by emphasizing our frailty and God's superiority. We wither like grass, and like flowers, our beauty fades. Contrastingly, the Lord never faints and never grows weary. Behold your God in His superiority!

5) The Lord is Eternal (Isaiah 40:8)

"…The grass withereth, the flower fadeth: but the word of our God shall stand forever."

His Word is an extension of His character. He has given His Word and His promises; and they shall stand forever. This is a tremendous comfort in times of trial and uncertainty. Behold your God in His eternality!

6) The Lord is Strong (Isaiah 40:10)

"Behold, the Lord GOD will come with strong hand, and his arm shall rule for him."

The One who can renew your strength is Himself a supply of never-ending strength. There is lasting security to be found in the strong hand of the Lord. For example, when you were falling asleep as a child you might have been comforted by the thought that, if someone were to come into your home in the night, your father was strong enough to defend your family. Likewise, as an adult in the midst of uncertainty, remember, "My heavenly Father is strong." Behold your God in His strength!

7) The Lord is Tender (Isaiah 40:11)

"He shall feed his flock like a shepherd: he shall gather the lambs with his arm, and carry them in his bosom, and shall gently lead those that are with young."

A tender intimacy is described here. The gentle guidance of our divine Shepherd, and the intimacy of His protective bosom provide a tender place of refuge in moments of panic and seasons of despair. Behold your God in His tenderness!

8) The Lord is Big (Isaiah 40:12)

"Who hath measured the waters in the hollow of his hand, and meted out heaven with the span, and comprehended the dust of the earth in a measure, and weighed the mountains in scales, and the hills in a balance?"

These rhetorical questions are designed to provoke us to thought. The problems we face often feel big, yet Isaiah wants us to see that the Lord is bigger than our problems.

His hand is capable of measuring the ocean waters in its hollow. Just like we cup water in our hands at a faucet so is the Lord big enough to cup the oceans in His hand. The distance from His thumb to His outstretched pinky finger represents the span of His hand and, in that span, the heavens and the galaxies are meted out. The mountains are big to us, but God is so big that He can set the mountains in scales and the hills in a balance. When we consider the magnitude of the Lord, it helps us realize that our problems are not as big as they seem. Behold your God in His bigness!

9) The Lord is All-Knowing (Isaiah 40:13-14)

"Who hath directed the Spirit of the LORD, or being his counsellor hath taught him? With whom took he counsel, and who instructed him, and taught him in the path of judgment, and taught him knowledge, and shewed to him the way of understanding?"

Again, rhetorical questions are used to provoke us to think about an attribute of the Lord. The LORD needs no one to teach Him. He is the "Wonderful Counselor" of Isaiah 9:6. He's all-knowing; He needs no outside information. Behold your God for His all-knowing nature!

10) The Lord is King (Isaiah 40:15-17)

"Behold, the nations are as a drop of a bucket."

So much of the background of Isaiah involves kings. For example, verse 23 speaks of princes and judges. Isaiah wants you to remember that the LORD is superior to all civil authority. He is the King of kings. Notice later in verse 15 that the nations "are counted as the small dust of the balance: behold, he taketh up the isles as a very little thing."

As King of kings, the Lord has resources far superior to any earthly king. Behold your God as King!

11) The Lord is Incomparable (Isaiah 40:18, 25)

"To whom then will ye liken God? or what likeness will ye compare unto him?"

God personally asks the question in verse 25: "To whom then will ye liken me, or shall I be equal? saith the Holy One." The answer, of course, is no one. He is incomparable. Behold your incomparable God!

12) The Lord is God (Isaiah 40:19-25)

"The workman melteth a graven image, and the goldsmith spreadeth it over with gold, and casteth silver chains. He that is so impoverished that he hath no oblation chooseth a tree that will not rot; he seeketh unto him a cunning workman to prepare a graven image, that shall not be moved. Have ye not known? have ye not heard? hath it not been told you from the beginning? have ye not understood from the foundations of the earth? It is he that sitteth upon the circle of the earth, and the inhabitants thereof are as grasshoppers; that stretcheth out the heavens as a curtain, and spreadeth them out as a tent to dwell in: That bringeth the princes to nothing; he maketh the judges of the earth as vanity. Yea, they shall not be planted; yea, they shall not be sown: yea, their stock shall not take root in the earth: and he shall also blow upon them, and they shall wither, and the whirlwind shall take them away as stubble. To whom then will ye liken me, or shall I be equal? saith the Holy One."

So often people either exalt themselves as God, or they craft some kind of idol. Notice that God addresses idolatry in verse 19. In that situation, the idol is a graven image made with gold or cast with silver chains. Verse 20 presents a different situation. Maybe the worshiper doesn't have the money for an idol that's gold or silver. He's in an economically depressed condition, and all he can do is create a wooden idol. He makes it out of a tree.

However, observe the contrast in verses 21-22: "Have ye not known? have ye not heard? hath it not been told you from the beginning? have ye not understood from the foundations of the earth? It is he that sitteth upon the circle of the earth, and the inhabitants thereof are as grasshoppers; that stretcheth out the heavens as a curtain, and spreadeth them out as a tent to dwell in."

While people try to worship all kinds of nonsense, the LORD is truly God. Again, the counselor Isaiah is just giving us the proper perspective. In the midst of crisis, Isaiah's instruction is to "Behold your God" (verse 9). In verse 26, his command is to "lift up your eyes on high" and see that this LORD, who is God, is your Creator and Sustainer.

Isaiah 40:28 summarizes the content of the chapter by reiterating several aspects of God's character. This is, again, specifically a response to the complaint against God in Isaiah 40:27.

In this verse, he is essentially saying, "Have you forgotten that our everlasting, creator God never gets tired and possesses unsearchable understanding? **Your way is not hidden from the Lord. Your cause has not been disregarded.**"

They needed renewed strength desperately; but in order for them to receive it, they needed to be reminded of who the Lord is. Before they can "wait on the LORD," they must reflect on who He is, not just how they feel about the Lord in the moments of their distress.

When facing times of uncertainty whether political, relational, financial, physical or all of the above, Isaiah wants us to remember that the LORD is holy, willful, glorious, superior, eternal, strong, tender, big, all-knowing, King, incomparable; and the LORD is God.

When we rehearse those attributes, we can begin to understand why He is worth "waiting on."

"They that wait upon the LORD shall…" Before we receive the promise of renewed strength, we must have a correct view of the Provider of that promise. Praise the Lord for His never-changing character.

the Wait

But they that WAIT upon the LORD…." (Isaiah 40:31a).

This verse can be summed up with two words: requirement and reward. The requirement is to "wait upon the LORD," and the reward is that our strength will be renewed. So often in our flesh, we want the reward without meeting the requirement. We live in an "I want it now" culture.

People say, "I want renewed strength now! I want to soar like an eagle now! I want to run and not be weary, and I want the reward of walking without fainting right now!"

Waiting, even waiting on the Lord, seems like an inconvenience to most people. We want the boundless spiritual activity and tireless energy described in this verse right now, but first, the requirement is to "wait upon the Lord."

When I think of the "I want it now" culture, my mind goes to the 1971 film, *"Willy Wonka and The Chocolate Factory."* The little girl in the film wanted everything now. One theme of the film is that entitled, impatient people are not to be rewarded. She did not understand the idea of waiting and, as a result, she was labeled a "bad egg" and fell down the incinerator chute with her enabling father right behind her.

The idea of waiting upon the Lord does have to do with God's timing, but it is more about trusting God. These two concepts, timing and trusting, go hand in hand. They are distinct from one another yet in some ways they're inseparable.

To be specific, the Hebrew phrase "wait upon" in Isaiah 40:31 means **"to bind together."** Waiting upon the Lord is to be "bound together" with God. It's a picture of complete trust even in the face of uncertain circumstances.

One Biblical example of this is Shadrach, Meshach, and Abednego. These guys knew what it meant to wait on the Lord. They were clearly **bound together with God.** Sometimes God doesn't keep you from the fire, but instead He enters into the fire with you.

Daniel 3:1 says, "Nebuchadnezzar the king made an image of gold, whose height was threescore cubits, and the breadth thereof six cubits: he set it up in the plain of Dura, in the province of Babylon." It was ninety feet tall and nine feet wide. In Daniel 3:6, the command is given that "Whoso falleth not down and worshippeth shall the same hour be cast into the midst of a burning fiery furnace." In other words, they were to worship the golden image, and if they didn't, they would face death by cremation.

It was reported to the king that these three Hebrew children would not worship the golden image, so "Nebuchadnezzar, in his rage and fury, commanded to bring Shadrach, Meshach and

Abednego to him."

The king engaged them in a bit of a dialog which revealed their trust in the Lord in the face of life-threatening adversity.

Daniel 3:14 says, "Nebuchadnezzar spake and said unto them, Is it true, O Shadrach, Meshach, and Abednego, do not ye serve my gods, nor worship the golden image which I have set up?" In verse 16, "Shadrach, Meshach, and Abednego, answered and said to the king, O Nebuchadnezzar, we are not careful to answer thee in this matter." In other words, they were not worried or panicked. Do you know why?

Shadrach, Meshach, and Abednego **were bound together with the Lord.** Whatever life allowed, they were going to "wait on the Lord," and therefore, they were not worried.

In Daniel 3:17, their answer continues. "If it be so, our God whom we serve is able to deliver us from the burning fiery furnace, and he will deliver us out of thine hand, O king. But if not, be it known unto thee, O king, that we will not serve thy gods, nor worship the golden image which thou hast set up."

No matter what, they were going to trust God. No matter what, they were going to "wait on the Lord." They declared that they would trust Him whether He delivered them from the trial or not because they were bound up together with Him.

Daniel 3:27 reveals that God protected them and that "the fire had no power, nor was an hair of their head singed, neither were their coats changed, nor the smell of fire had passed on them."

They met the requirement of waiting on the Lord, and they reaped the reward of renewed strength!

Can you imagine them coming out of that furnace? What excitement! What joy! Certainly, in that moment they experienced renewed strength and likely felt like they could "mount up with wings as eagles; run and not be weary; and walk and not faint."

To put it in a New Testament way, they must've felt like "more than conquerors," after trusting in the Lord through that horrific trial.

Another Biblical example of what it means to "wait on the Lord" is found in Daniel 6. Daniel had the holy habit of praying to God at his window three times per day. In spite of a conspiratorial decree to the contrary, Daniel continued this habit. As a result, Daniel faced the consequence of being thrown into a den of lions. Famously, God sent His angels to shut the lions' mouths so that Daniel would not be hurt. The Bible indicates that throughout this entire experience, "Daniel believed in his God." (Daniel 6:23). Daniel **trusted** in God. He **waited** on the Lord. Daniel was **bound together** with God.

Much like Shadrach, Meshach and Abednego, imagine how Daniel must've felt as he was being taken up out of the lions' den completely unharmed. After meeting the requirement of waiting on the Lord and trusting in God's timing, Daniel reaped the reward of renewed strength. The requirement is trust.

Proverbs 3:5-6 sum up the idea of "waiting on the Lord" perfectly. "Trust in the Lord with all thine heart; and lean not unto thine own understanding. In all thy ways acknowledge him, and he shall direct thy paths."

Occasionally in my preaching and writing, I will use Scripture references in a verb form. This is one of those times. Whatever you're facing, "Proverbs 3:5-6" it.

Let me ask you this: Will you Proverbs 3:5-6 your situation? Will you WAIT on the Lord? What is your situation of suffering, your situation of uncertainty? You want that renewed strength? **The requirement is to trust in the Lord with all your heart.**

You will never enjoy the beauty of renewed strength until you wait. You will never enjoy the spiritual ecstasy of effortlessly soaring like an eagle until you tarry for a moment in the presence and comfort of your heavenly Father.

I hope you have reflected on the character of God, and the twelve attributes of the Lord listed in Isaiah 40 because He is the One who is worth the wait.

Waiting on the Lord is required before you get your strength renewed. The question is "Will you wait?" But to put it a different way, "Are you bound together with God?"

the Strength

"But they that wait upon the LORD shall renew their strength." (Isaiah 40:31)

Remember the situation into which Isaiah writes. Sennacherib, the king of Assyria, had invaded Israel. The temple was desecrated, and Jerusalem had been taken over. One reason that God's prophet, Isaiah, explains the offer of renewed strength is that these people clearly needed it. They were overwhelmed with the uncertainty of their circumstance. This life-or-death situation had reminded them of their frailty.

One would think that this situation would have brought these people to their knees in humble prayer, yet the people of God were found complaining. As we studied previously, Isaiah 40:27 reveals the people's complaint toward God.

"Why sayest thou, O Jacob, and speakest, O Israel, My way is hid from the LORD, and my judgment is passed over from my God?"

Instead of turning to God for help in humility, they were complaining. Remember, they felt as though God wasn't seeing them anymore, as if He had abandoned them. Their complaint was that they felt like their cause had been disregarded by God.

Please notice the pride in their complaint. In spite of the desperation of their circumstance, they still had the audacity to tell God how to be God. They thought God should make Himself known to them, or they thought God should advocate for their cause, or they thought God should do any number of things. Instead of saying "God, I am your servant," they were acting as if God were their servant.

This is a common mentality among Christians today. People treat God like an errand boy. They expect Him to accomplish their personal ambitions and, if God doesn't, they decide they will not serve Him anymore. These people probably aren't actually serving God in the first place.

A spiritually mature Christian loves God not for what He can do for him, but for who He is. This is why Isaiah spends so much of chapter 40 explaining the character of the Lord. He wants these people to love the Lord because He is the "everlasting God, the LORD, the Creator of the ends of the earth."

Isaiah is teaching them, and us, to not just love the Lord because He has the power to rescue us from our trials but to love Him even if He doesn't rescue us. Love Him for who He is. Love Him because He is the Lord, and we are privileged to be His servants.

Because they still possessed enough pride to complain, Isaiah endeavored to promote the pursuit of humility by reminding them of their weakness in Isaiah 40:6-8. They were already feeling weak, but Isaiah knew that for them to have renewed strength they must be empty of pride, empty of ego, and empty of self.

The New Testament says it this way, "Humble yourselves in the sight of the Lord, and he shall lift you up." (James 4:10)

Renewed strength only comes when we are willing to exchange our strength for His strength. This is the idea of the word "renew" in Isaiah 40:31. It is a contrast between something new and something old. In this text, **"renew" literally means "to change or exchange."**

This is what it means when God says "…my strength is made perfect in weakness," in 2 Corinthians 12:9. His renewed strength will only be perfected in us when we get to the point of thoroughly recognizing our weakness, and therefore, our desperate need for Him.

Unfortunately, many people, even Christians, are content to live with the temporal things that make them feel strong.

Psalm 52:7 explains it like this, "Lo, this is the man that made not God his strength; but trusted in the abundance of his riches and strengthened himself in his wickedness."

We also read in Proverbs 18:11 that, "The rich man's wealth is his strong city, and as an high wall in his own conceit." It's as if man can build an unscalable wall around his life over which his problems cannot climb.

Jeremiah 9:23 gives us a summary statement of things in which we often find our human strength. "Thus saith the LORD, Let not the wise man glory in his wisdom, neither let the mighty man glory in his might, let not the rich man glory in his riches."

The Lord essentially says, "Don't source your strength in your mental ability (wisdom), or your physical muscles (might), or your money (riches). Don't glory in your mental acuity, your muscles, or your money." One old preacher said it this way, "Don't boast in your brains, your brawn, or your bucks!"

That doesn't mean that it's wrong to pursue knowledge by getting good grades or advanced degrees. It doesn't mean that it's wrong to exercise and try to be physically fit and strong. The Lord is not saying that it's wrong to have money, but He is saying that a man that possesses wisdom will not boast in these things.

The wise person will not source his strength in these things but instead he will source his strength in the Provider and Sustainer of these things.

We are all only stewards of any mental, physical, or financial resources that we may possess. It all belongs to God. The Apostle Paul is an amazing example of someone who understood this idea of renewed strength.

If Paul were to glory or boast, he would not glory in the things from which people typically draw their strength. In 2 Corinthians 11:30 Paul explains, "If I must needs glory, I will glory of the things which concern mine infirmities." Infirmities are weaknesses.

In 2 Corinthians 12:9-10, Paul famously explains "Most gladly therefore will I rather glory in my infirmities, that the power of Christ may rest upon me." Paul understands the EXCHANGE!

He understands the "renewed strength" explained in Isaiah 40:31. Paul said, "I take pleasure in infirmities, in reproaches, in necessities, in persecutions, in distresses for Christ's sake: for when I am weak, then am I strong."

Instead of sinfully complaining about weaknesses or complaining in our situations of uncertainty, let us "take pleasure" in these moments, because it is then that the "power (strength) of Christ may rest upon us." Renewed strength is exchanging our perceived strength, which is only temporal, for His potent strength, which is eternal.

the Activity

"...they shall mount up with wings as eagles; they shall run, and not be weary; and they shall walk, and not faint." (Isaiah 40:31b)

Mounting up with wings as eagles, running and not being weary, and walking without fainting are each metaphorical pictures. They are invigorating illustrations, specifically included to help us understand the preceding instruction.

The first part of Isaiah 40:31 is the instruction, "…they that wait upon the LORD shall renew their strength" while the latter portion of the verse is the illustration of that instruction.

The activities described in that latter part of the verse illustrate the reward that only comes after our strength is renewed. The requirement is to wait on the Lord and the reward is renewed strength and zeal for life.

Let's consider each of these three illustrations.

"Mount Up with Wings as Eagles"

Eagles soar with an efficient, effortless, and elegant style. The idea of Isaiah 40:31 is that, because I know who the Lord is and because I know how to trust/wait on Him and because I have exchanged my feeble strength for His divine strength, I then can face uncertain circumstances with an efficient, effortless, and elegant disposition.

The illustration of this beautiful spiritual mindset stands in contrast to a mindset that might be illustrated by many other creatures. Isaiah, moved by the Holy Ghost of God, deliberately picked an eagle. For example, he did not pick a hummingbird even though many Christians conduct themselves more like hummingbirds than eagles.

The hummingbird's wing beats are among the most energy intensive in the animal kingdom. They look panicked and frantic much like we do when we face trials.

The hummingbird is also the only bird that can fly backwards. Often people spend too much time being defined by the past instead of living presently for the Lord and looking to the future for Christ's imminent return.

Additionally, the hummingbird typically travels alone. The Jews of Isaiah's day felt like they were all alone and hidden from God; we often feel alone in our times of trial. Isaiah 40:31 does not use the frantic looking, backward flying, self-isolating hummingbird as its illustration. Instead, Isaiah wants us to see the picture of an efficient, effortless, and elegant eagle flying above the turbulence of life.

"Run and Not Be Weary"

Could you imagine running like an ultra-marathon runner? These athletes seem to run endlessly without growing weary. I have recently taken up cross country running. My son runs on his high school's cross country team, and he gave me some very helpful advice.

He said, "Father, run your race." He explained to me that there are many differing factors among runners. It is unrealistic to think that I could keep up with someone who weighs significantly less than I do. After all, while they may be running on the same course, they are carrying a lot less weight. Also, it is unrealistic to think that a man in his forties could keep up with cross country runners in their twenties.

The key to running and not being weary includes, "running YOUR race." It's wise to avoid comparing yourself to other people as they run their race. The writer of Hebrews instructs us to "run with patience the race that is set before us." It is just as my son said, "Run your race."

Another key to not growing weary is this: while you're running your race, keep "looking unto Jesus the author and finisher of our faith." (Hebrews 12:2)

The reason that we are to look to Jesus is that He is no stranger to suffering. The Bible explains that Jesus, "for the joy that was set before him endured the cross, despising the shame, and is set down at the right hand of the throne of God."

He went through the difficulty of the cross and then enjoyed the reward of being set down at the right hand of the throne of God. Certain successes are only experienced if we keep running in spite of temporal suffering, all the while, "Looking unto Jesus."

"Walk and Not Faint"

The Bible often uses walking as a metaphor for spiritual progress. Ephesians 5:15 instructs us to, "walk circumspectly," and Galatians 5:16 explains that we are to "walk in the Spirit."

Psalm 23:4 comforts us as we "walk through the valley of the shadow of death." The sorrow that accompanies losing a loved one to death can be a journey that can cause fainting. Yet the Psalmist reminds us that our Shepherd leads us through "paths of righteousness," and that's why no matter the depth of the valley we "will fear no evil" for He is with us.

Herein is the key to walking and not fainting. Since He is with us, there is no reason to faint. Goodness and mercy are following the believer all the days of his life.

The Jewish people of Isaiah's day needed to be reminded of who the Lord is. God's prophet beautifully illustrated the reward of waiting on the Lord. These activities, mounting up with wings as eagles, running without being weary, walking and not fainting, can be the spiritual mindset of every faithful follower of Christ.

Understanding and applying each ingredient described in Isaiah 40:31 is essential to receiving the invigorating power of renewed strength. Each day of the Christian's earthly journey requires not only a reflection on the Lord, but also the wait, the strength, and the activity.

Conclusion

The major point of chapter 40 is that weak, struggling people, as we all are, need to assess their view of God and make certain it's a Biblical view.

We need to see God for who He is and not allow our view of God to be skewed by our emotions as we face the inevitable panic that often accompanies the many struggles of life.

Isaiah says to weak, struggling people, "Behold Your God!" (Isaiah 40:9)

That's the only way renewed strength comes. It comes when we see and know God, and the only way to do that is to cling to what His Word declares about His character.

In Isaiah 40:26 he says, "Lift up your eyes on high, and behold."

The way to behold God is to read, apply, and love His Word. We are weak, yet He disperses His renewed strength through that which shall stand forever; **His Word.**

The key to understanding Isaiah 40:31 is to understand and apply Isaiah 40:8. (See also Joshua 1:8-9)

The apostle Peter understood this. That's why he quotes Isaiah 40:8 in 1 Peter 1:24, 25. Peter writes to Christians facing serious trial and possible death as martyrs for their faith in Christ.

So, what is a person to do if he wants renewed strength? Turn to the **Word of God.**

What is a person to do if he wants to help other struggling people have renewed strength? Do what Isaiah instructed (Isaiah 40:9) and what Peter did: point them to the Word of God. In the midst of whatever chaos you face, be comforted (Isaiah 40:1) by the eternality of God's Word and the reliability of His promises.

Therein is the goal of this book. Over and over again *Renewed Strength* has quoted and referenced the Word of God because that's where "good success" is found (Joshua 1:8-9).

If this copy of *Renewed Strength* strengthened you in your walk with God and your love for the Bible, we would like to hear from you. Email our ministry at contact@strengthforlife.church.

Isaiah's Song of Strength

Isaiah 26:3-4

"Thou wilt keep him in perfect peace, whose mind is stayed on thee: because he trusteth in thee. Trust ye in the LORD for ever: for in the LORD JEHOVAH is everlasting strength:" (Isaiah 26:3-4)

Times of trial are real, and often they're painful. Emotional, physical, mental and even spiritual pain can accompany certain trials.

Trials are also universal. Your big bank balance will not keep you from trials. Neither will your popularity, notoriety, or personality keep you from times of trouble.

Trials come to everyone. No one escapes the "thorns and thistles" of life. Trials are universally a part of the human condition. Sometimes we bring trials on ourselves, while other times the trials are no fault of our own. Yet, either way, we're faced with it.

How marvelous it is that Christians don't face trials alone! The Creator God of the universe offers aid to His children that the world does not receive. This help is exclusively available to those who know Christ as Savior.

From Isaiah 26:3-4 we will see the supply, the source, the stipulation, the security and the song.

First, consider the supply.

Isaiah 26:3-4 explains that "perfect peace" and "everlasting strength" can be supplied to the children of God. It's a two-fold supply that goes hand-in-hand.

Throughout life, peace and strength are often coupled together. A spiritually strong person is calm in the Lion's dens of life. He is at peace when the flames of the fiery furnace surround him.

By contrast, panic is seen as weakness.

In Isaiah 26, God is saying that you can be supplied with peace and strength in the midst of any trial, and you don't have to panic and walk in weakness!

The peace is "perfect peace," which is to say, "peace peace." In the Hebrew of Isaiah 26:3 it's "Shalom, Shalom." It's the word "peace" twice. You could say it's double peace. "Perfect peace" is the idea of wholeness or complete peace. It is the perfect peace through which we can face whatever trial that comes into our lives.

The strength supplied in Isaiah 26:4 is "everlasting strength." The Hebrew word for everlasting carries with it the idea of "no vanishing point." It's eternal, perpetual strength. It's limitless strength. It's without end.

Whatever you're facing, the Word of God promises that, "you can be supplied with perfect peace and everlasting strength!"

Second, consider the source of the supply.

The God of heaven is the source of this "perfect peace" and "everlasting strength."

In Isaiah 26:3-4, notice how many times God is referred to, in either pronoun or noun form.

"Thou wilt keep him …"
"…whose mind is stayed on **thee."**
"because he trusteth in **thee."**
"Trust ye in the **LORD** for ever."
"for in the **LORD JEHOVAH** is …"

The source of the supply is Jehovah God. Remember, He is the One who spoke the world into existence. He is the One who breathed life into man. He is the One who sustains all the galaxies and specifically, He is the One who sustains your beating heart.

When someone writes you a personal check, it's only as good as the signature on the bottom. Here, the source of this heavenly promise of peace and strength is Almighty God! His truth doesn't change. His Word is forever settled. He is the One with whom there "is no variableness neither shadow of turning."

Third, consider the stipulation.

Verse three explains that God will "keep him in perfect peace, whose mind is stayed on thee." The stipulation is that your mind is "stayed" on God. It's the idea of being steadfast. It means to be rooted and grounded in God. Metaphorically, it's to be anchored or riveted on God. The word "stayed" specifically means to remain in place.

If you're a dog owner, maybe you've worked with your canine and taught him some tricks. Possibly you've taught your dog to sit on command, or to speak by barking. When we are visiting someone's home, and they have a well-trained dog, we respect it. When the pet owner instructs their dog to sit, and then stay, to remain in place, we respect the discipline of the dog as he obeys his master. Isaiah 26 is instructing us that if we want perfect peace, and everlasting strength, in a world full of trials, our heavenly Master tells us to remain in place and have our mind "stayed" on Him.

Often, the trials that we face seem like they're messing with our mind. Do you find yourself full of anxiety and mental and emotional panic? God says to focus your mind on Him! He says to anchor your inner man on His divine character and His eternal word! This is the stipulation.

Fourthly, consider the security of Isaiah 26:3.

"Thou wilt keep…" The word "keep" means to guard, protect, and maintain. It's a military term. The imagery here is of a soldier who is posted to guard or keep a specific area. It's his responsibility to keep that area secure. He is standing guard against the stealthy advance of an enemy. When we meet the stipulation and our mind is stayed on Him, then God is on guard on our behalf!

Interestingly, in the New Testament, it's very likely that when the apostle Paul wrote Philippians 4:6-7, he had Isaiah 26:3 in mind. Notice the similarities.

"Be careful for nothing; but in every thing by prayer and supplication with thanksgiving let your requests be made known unto God. And the peace of God, which passeth all understanding, shall keep your hearts and minds through Christ Jesus."

Finally, consider the song.

Isaiah 26:1 makes it clear that this chapter is a song. It's a song of encouragement and jubilance in the midst of trial.

And, from Isaiah's song of strength in Isaiah 26, other songs have been written. Frances Ridley Havergal penned "Like A River Glorious" with Isaiah 26 in mind.

Frances was an amazingly gifted poet and lyrical writer who lived in the mid 1800's. She was a P.K; a preacher's kid. Frances never married, but she mastered many languages. She was saved at 15 years old when her father led her to Christ. She fell in love with Jesus and spent her life writing about Him. At 39 years old, while in South Wales, she caught a severe cold and suffered the inflammation of her lungs. It was then that a doctor told her she only had a short time to live. He explained that she would soon die. Indeed, Frances did die at the young age of 42 years old. But, somewhere between her diagnosis at 39 and her death at 42, Frances penned that well-known hymn, "Like A River Glorious."

In that hymn, she beautifully describes the "perfect peace" and "everlasting strength" that God supplied for her.

Frances writes,

"Like a river glorious Is God's perfect peace,
Over all victorious In its bright increase;
Perfect, yet it floweth Fuller ev'ry day;
Perfect, yet it groweth Deeper all the way.

Hidden in the hollow Of His blessed hand,
Never foe can follow, Never traitor stand;
Not a surge of worry, Not a shade of care,
Not a blast of hurry Touch the spirit there.

Refrain:

Stayed upon Jehovah, Hearts are fully blest -
Finding as He promised, Perfect peace and rest."
Frances' friends and family said that to the end, she kept her mind
stayed on Jehovah. To the end, she exhibited "perfect peace" and
"everlasting strength."

May God help us to have our minds stayed on Him and to "trust
in the Lord forever," so that we will receive "perfect peace" and
"everlasting strength" as we face the turbulence and the trials of
life.

A Psalm of Strength

Psalm 46:1-11

If we take a quick snapshot of the world today, we read of trouble such as the terrorism in Afghanistan. Suicide bombers killed 13 U.S. military members and as a result, Gold Star families are seen weeping on live television over the loss of their children.

As I write this, people around the world are battling the coronavirus and struggling with serious sickness.

Over the last year and a half, we have heard countless stories of lockdowns and individual rights being infringed upon by local and federal governments.

We see hurricanes. Ida is hitting the gulf coast today as I write this, and of course on this same day 16 years ago Hurricane Katrina struck New Orleans.

If you look into our specific section of the snapshot, within our own church, people are facing trouble of various types. Many of our church folks have been praying for a godly lady in our church as she faces liver transplant surgery. Others have recently lost a loved one to death, and their heart is grieving.

Some in our congregation have struggled financially due to a loss of employment. Now feelings of financial insecurity overwhelm their soul.

Psalm 46 is a song of strength in a world full of trouble.

So much of what we're facing today is the same type of thing that the Psalmist was facing in his day.

In light of today's troubles, consider the timelessly relevant help that God provides in Psalm 46.

Notice how the Psalmist describes God, trouble, gladness, power and then God Himself prescribes solutions to the troubles we face.

1. Describing God (vs 1)

"God is our refuge and strength, a very present help in trouble." (Psalm 46:1)

Consider how the Psalmist describes God. He explains that God is "a refuge and strength, a very present help…"

The word "refuge" carries the idea of shelter, but the word also means fortress. As our refuge, He's not just a rickety tin roof that keeps you out of the rain but could blow off with a strong gust of wind. He's more than that. He is our fortress. As our refuge, He is a robust shelter, a solid fortress.

"Strength" in this text is not just strong, but the strongest.

Specifically, in our weakness, He is "our strength." It's relational. We can depend on Him because He is "our strength."

Further, God is our "help." In times of trouble, the psalmist says you can cry out to God as your help.

But He's not just help; He's "present help."

When you need help, in most cases, you want someone present with you. God is "present help."

But He is not present in that He is in the same house with you but staying in the room down the hall. No! He is "very present help."

He is right next to you, in the same room where you are. You can identify His presence, and benefit from His help immediately.

"The Lord of hosts is with us" (vs 7 & 11).

"Therefore" (vs 2) or with the understanding that God is our refuge and strength, a very present help in trouble, now we know that we have nothing to fear!

Now that this song of strength has reminded us who God is, we are much better prepared to face trouble.

2. Describing Trouble (vs 2-3)

"Therefore will not we fear, though the earth be removed, and though the mountains be carried into the midst of the sea; Though the waters thereof roar and be troubled, though the mountains shake with the swelling thereof. Selah." (Psalm 46:2-3)

What if "the earth be removed"? What if "the mountains be carried into the midst of the sea"? What if "the waters thereof roar and be troubled"?

By the way, why would the waters thereof roar and be troubled as described in verse 3? It's because in verse 2 the mountains were just carried and dropped into the midst of the sea!

What if "the mountains shake with the swelling thereof"? (This is a reference to earthquakes).

Even if these things happen, the Psalmist is saying, "No need to be alarmed. We have nothing to fear." Why? Because again, "God is our refuge and strength, a very present help in trouble." Realizing those amazing truths brings gladness into this song of strength.

3. Describing Gladness (vs 4-5)

"There is a river, the streams whereof shall make glad the city of God, the holy place of the tabernacles of the most High. God is in the midst of her; she shall not be moved: God shall help her, and that right early." (Psalm 46:4-5)

Verses four and five are contrasting verses to two and three. Trouble is described in two and three, while gladness is pictured in four and five. Specifically, a glad city. The refreshing waters and the peaceful stream bring glad thoughts as the Psalmist describes the "city of God." The most comforting element of that city is that "God is in the midst of her." Interestingly the most beautiful aspect of heaven is not the golden streets or the gates of pearl, but it is the light of that city, God Himself, the Lord Jesus Christ. Dwelling with Him forever in perfection and harmony brings gladness to the mind of every child of God.

4. Describing God's Power (vs 6-9)

"The heathen raged, the kingdoms were moved: he uttered his

voice, the earth melted. The LORD of hosts is with us; the God of Jacob is our refuge. Selah. Come, behold the works of the LORD, what desolations he hath made in the earth. He maketh wars to cease unto the end of the earth; he breaketh the bow, and cutteth the spear in sunder; he burneth the chariot in the fire." (Psalm 46:6-9)

In this song of strength God's power is described. Specifically, His powerful voice is louder (vs 6), His powerful army is larger (vs 7) and His powerful works are limiting (vs 8-9).

Notice that His voice is louder in verse 6. The loud raging heathen may move kingdoms on the earth, but if God merely utters His voice, the earth could melt. God's powerful voice is louder.

Consider that His powerful army is larger in verse 7. The phrase, "The Lord of hosts" is one of God's many names. In Hebrew the "Lord of hosts" is the Lord "Sabaoth," which means "a mass of persons organized for war." To say that He is "The Lord of hosts" is to say, that He is "The Lord of armies." He has His universe of resources at His disposal to defeat any opposing military forces.

There are hundreds of names or titles for God in the Bible which help describe who God is and those names also bring us comfort. For example, "Adonai" means that God is Master and Lord of all. "Elohim" means that He is our covenant keeping creator God. "El Shaddai" indicates that He is the almighty powerful One.

Victoriously in verse 7 He is the Lord of hosts, the Lord Sabaoth. His powerful armies are larger than His enemies and therefore He is the One who can make "wars cease" vs 9.

As we continue to sing this song of strength, notice in verses 8-9 that His works are limiting. He wants us to "Behold the works of the LORD." Behold means to see. The Psalmist wants us to see with our mind's eye the amazing ways in which God's works are able to limit His enemies.

He wants us to see "what desolations he hath made in the earth." The word "desolations" means astonishment and wonder, but it also describes "things that God brings to ruin and waste." The Psalmist is saying, "See the astonishing ways in which God limits His enemies. Behold with wonder how He brings to ruin their wicked ambitions." He may have Sennacherib and the Assyrians in view here but certainly this truth applies to any of the self-appointed enemies of God.

When they shoot their bow, thrust their spear, or charge in their chariot, the Psalmist explains that the Lord of hosts has the power to break their bow, cut their spear, and burn their chariot.

All of these poetic war metaphors are symbolic of the various troubles of life. Do you see the acceleration and progression of verse 9? Like when you push down the gas pedal in an automobile, you begin to go faster and faster, the acceleration can be exhilarating. In verse 9, your heart is beating quickly thinking about the arrow from the bow that almost stabbed you, then the spear that almost sliced you, and then the chariot that almost trampled you!

As your heart races with exhilaration and potential fear from verse 9, that's when God says, "Be still" in verse 10.

Problems are swarming all around you and threatening your livelihood and maybe even your life, and then God speaks plainly, "Be still."

Notice that the voice in this song of strength changes. In verses one through nine, the Psalmist is speaking about God, but in verse 10, God Himself speaks!

5. Prescribing Solutions (vs 10-11)

"Be still, and know that I am God: I will be exalted among the heathen, I will be exalted in the earth. The LORD of hosts is with us; the God of Jacob is our refuge. Selah." (Psalm 46:10-11)

In verse 10 God gives us two specific instructions. He prescribes two solutions to the many troubles of life.

He says, "Be still" and then He says, "know" some things. The instruction to "Be still" is a call to take a position of strength. When the arrow flies by, when the spear is thrust, when the chariot is traveling quickly in your direction, the temptation is to bob-and-weave or to run for cover. The temptation is to panic, yet here, God says, "Be still." He is saying, "Stand strong. Stand in My strength. Rest calmly in My refuge. Be still in Me."

But, don't "be still" in ignorance. Secondly, He instructs the believer to "know" some things. Notice that He doesn't say to "feel" some things. Instead of being led by your emotions and feelings in times of trouble, you must ruminate on some specific things. You must rest on certain eternal verities.

Know that He is God. Know that He will be exalted among the heathen, and that He will be exalted in the earth.

Know that "the LORD of hosts is with us" and that "the God of Jacob is our refuge." The Lord of armies is with us. As our refuge He is our shelter and fortress.

Then this song of strength concludes with the word, "Selah." Three times in the text we read this word. (At the end of vs 3, vs 7, and verse 11).

Charles H. Spurgeon explains in "The Treasury of David" that Selah is, "rest in contemplation after praise."

He says, "It is easier to sing a hymn of praise than to continue in the spirit of praise, but let it be our aim to maintain the uprising devotion of our grateful hearts, and so end our song as if we intended it to be continued."

"Selah bids the music rest
Pause in silence soft and blest
Selah bids uplift the strain
Harps and voices tune again
Selah ends the vocal praise
Still your hearts to God up raise."

Psalm 46 is certainly a song of strength in the midst of trouble, but interestingly, it is "A Song upon Alamoth."

Some commentators point out that this word "Alamoth" in the Hebrew has to do with "young maidens."

The speculation by many commentators is that "Alamoth" could be a technical musical notation indicating that this Psalm is a song that should be sung primarily by female voices because they have a higher range than most men.

Another interesting aspect of this Psalm is that Psalm 46 was Martin Luther's inspiration to pen the well-known hymn, "A Mighty Fortress Is Our God." Included in the lyrics, Martin Luther writes,

"Did we in our own strength confide,
Our striving would be losing;
Were not the right Man on our side,
The Man of God's own choosing:

Dost ask who that may be?
Christ Jesus, it is He –
Lord Sabaoth, His name,
From age to age the same-
And He must win the battle."

In the final verse Luther writes, "Let goods and kindred go, This mortal life also; The body they may kill: God's truth abideth still - His kingdom is forever."

Conclusion:

After reviewing Psalm 46, will you do as Spurgeon suggests? After singing this song of strength, will you let it continue? Just because the music director concludes the song and allows the audience to be seated, that doesn't mean that this song is over. Selah calls us to sing the song long after it has been sung. Will you continue to ruminate on the truths of Psalm 46 and rest in them as you face the troubles of life?

And, as Luther teaches in that hymn, will you prioritize God's Word and God's Kingdom over "goods and kindred"? Will you prioritize that which is eternal (God's Word and God's Kingdom) over this mortal life?

This song of strength helps us as it majestically describes God, trouble, gladness, and power. Then, it helps us as we rejoice when God Himself prescribes solutions to the numerous troubles we face on a daily basis. Psalm 46 is a beautiful Song of Strength!

A Prayer for Strength

Ephesians 3:14-21 records a prayer that the Apostle Paul prayed for the Ephesian believers. It's a prayer for God to grant them strength in their inner man, to give them renewed strength. When life is confusing and we're feeling weak, we often don't know how to pray. So, let's pray like the Apostle Paul.

Consider the purpose, posture, Person, petitions and the power of Paul's prayer for strength.

First, notice Paul's purpose in praying what he did. Verse 14 begins, "For this cause I bow my knees…" The purpose or "cause" of his prayer is explained in verse 13. His "desire" is "that ye faint not…." He's burdened that believers remain strong in their faith in Christ. In verse 12 he powerfully reminds them of the "boldness and access with confidence" they should have "by the faith of him." His cause or purpose in prayer is for God to strengthen believers at the core of who they are.

Secondly, notice Paul's posture in prayer. He says, "I bow my knees…." Various physical postures of prayer are mentioned in Scripture, yet none is necessarily better than the other. Whether you're kneeling, standing, sitting or even lying down, the key is the posture of your heart. Physically bowing your knees is symbolic of a humble spirit. However, people can physically bow while at the same time they have a raging rebellion in their heart. Whatever your physical prayer posture, be certain that the posture of your heart is a humble dependence on God. Your heart should not reflect an entitled or arrogant spirit, but instead your inner man should cry, "God, I need You. You are my Lord and Master and I humbly and dependently bow my heart to You and Your will." Paul's posture represents humility and a submissive spirit.

Thirdly, consider the Person to whom Paul prays. He prays "unto the Father of our Lord Jesus Christ." In that simple phrase, Paul touches on the divine nature of Jesus by describing the hypostatic union. He prays to God "the Father" who is the Father of "Jesus" of Nazareth (a term relating to His humanity) and he refers to Jesus as "Lord" and "Christ" (terms describing His divinity).

As Paul explains the individual personhood that Jesus possesses, a personhood distinct from His Father, Paul also mentions the equality Jesus has with His Father by calling Jesus "Lord." Additionally, Paul references Jesus' messiahship by identifying Him as "Christ." Paul is essentially saying, as he does often in his writings, "Unequivocally, Jesus is the anointed One!" All of this is an extremely thoughtful and respectful way to address the Person of God.

As Paul continues, he describes the Person of God to whom he prays as the One "of whom the whole family in heaven and earth is named." He is saying that he's invoking the same God as believers from past and current generations. Old Testament people like Abraham, along with other believers who had lived in previous generations, had long since died when Paul wrote Ephesians. Those believers were already part of the "whole family in heaven." Paul is saying, "I am praying to the same God that believers who are already in heaven prayed to, and I'm praying to the same God that believers currently on the earth are naming."

Fourthly, this brings us to Paul's petitions in prayer. "That he would grant you according to the riches of his glory…."

1) To be strengthened with might by His Spirit in the inner man;
2) That Christ may dwell in your hearts by faith;
3) That ye, being rooted and grounded in love, may be able to comprehend with all saints what is the breadth, and length, and depth, and height; (of that love)
4) And to know the love of Christ, which passeth knowledge,
5) That ye might be filled with all the fulness of God.

Notice that the petitions of his prayer emphasize a strengthening both emotionally and intellectually, of both heart and mind. Paul focuses his prayer on their "inner man," their "hearts," but he also prays that the Ephesians would "know" and "comprehend" things that pertain to the "love of Christ." Paul is aware of a believer's propensity toward disingenuous externalism; thus, his prayer focuses on the internal genuineness and intellectual awareness of their faith. Essentially, he's praying that they would be spiritually strengthened as they endeavor to love God with all their heart, soul, mind, and strength. (Matthew 22:34-40, Deut. 6:5, Mark 12:30)

Paul is praying that, in spite of whatever comes their way, that they would look at their temporal circumstances through the lens of what Christ has lovingly done for them. He wants them to be strong in genuinely seeing their lives through the lens of the eternality of the gospel. This realignment to a big picture gospel perspective is spiritually medicinal and can calm the panic that often accompanies times of crisis in this temporal life. Because, after all, "Christ is dwelling in [our] hearts by faith," so why fear? The presence of Christ in our hearts is a comforting prayer and needful reminder in any time of tribulation. (v 13)

Further, notice the trinitarian emphasis in the prayer. We are strengthened "by His Spirit" (v 16), and we are to know the "love of Christ" (v 19) and we are to "be filled with all the fullness of God." This prayer initially addresses the "Father" (v 14), yet it beautifully includes each member of the divine trinity.

As Paul begins to conclude his prayer, he recognizes a **power** much greater than his own human abilities provide. Paul says, **"Now unto him that is able to do exceeding abundantly above all that we ask or think, according to the power that worketh in us…."**

God is so powerful that He can do unfathomable things through us. Did you catch that? His mind-blowing power can work through **us.** The access to this kind of divine power has the potential to puff us up in pride, so Paul makes sure to humbly give God all the glory when he says, **"Unto him be glory in the church by Christ Jesus throughout all ages, world without end. Amen."**

Notice the phrase **"in the church."** When God grants this kind of renewed strength, a church is enabled to do amazing things in spite of the inevitable spiritual adversity.

"The gates of hell will not prevail against the church." (Matthew

16:18) And, it's in the church that He should receive all the glory!

Paul's prayer for spiritual strength should be prayed often. It's spiritually healthy to regularly rehearse Paul's purpose, posture, Person, petitions and power as described in Ephesians 3:14-21. May God divinely strengthen us "according to the riches of His glory by Christ Jesus."

After having read the above explanation of Ephesians 3:14-21, consider praying this Prayer for Strength…

(Note: In Ephesians 3, Paul is praying this prayer for others, but consider praying this prayer for yourself.)

"For this cause I bow my knees unto the Father of our Lord Jesus Christ, Of whom the whole family in heaven and earth is named, That he would grant [me], according to the riches of his glory, to be strengthened with might by his Spirit in the inner man; That Christ may dwell in [my heart] by faith; that [I would be] rooted and grounded in love, [and that I] may be able to comprehend with all saints what is the breadth, and length, and depth, and height; And [that I would] know the love of Christ, which passeth knowledge, that [I] might be filled with all the fulness of God. Now unto him that is able to do exceeding abundantly above all that we ask or think, according to the power that worketh in us, Unto him be glory in the church by Christ Jesus throughout all ages, world without end. Amen."

Final Thoughts

Before you enjoy the benefits of the Christian life, you must be sure you're a Christian. _Renewed Strength_ is for the Christian. Salvation is the foundation upon which the benefits of the Christian life are enjoyed. Please consider closely the following questions and Bible-based answers.

WHERE WILL YOU SPEND ETERNITY?

This is the most important question facing mankind. We are eternal beings and when we die our soul will spend eternity somewhere. Hebrews 9:27 tells us, "And as it is appointed unto men once to die, but after this the judgment." The Bible teaches that there are only two options – Heaven or Hell.

WHAT GETS ME TO HELL?

The bad news is, you don't have to do anything in order to spend eternity in Hell. Jesus said in John 3:18b, "but he that believeth not is condemned already, because he hath not believed in the name of the only begotten Son of God."

Whenever we break God's law it is sin and Romans 3:23 explains that our sin is the reason we face God's judgment – "For all have sinned and come short of the glory of God."

We are sinful people, and that sin has consequences. Romans 6:23a describes this punishment: "For the wages of sin is death." This means separation from God for all eternity. This indeed is bad news, but God has provided a way to escape sin's penalty.

WHAT GETS ME TO HEAVEN?

The good news is, God has provided a Substitute to die in our place: Jesus Christ. Romans 6:23b says "but the gift of God is eternal life through Jesus Christ our Lord."

God sent His perfect Son Jesus Christ to die on your behalf and pay sin's penalty. In John 3:16 Jesus said, "For God so loved the world, that He gave his only begotten Son, that whosoever believeth in Him should not perish, but have everlasting life."

Jesus Christ is the only way to Heaven; He died on the cross and rose again in order to pay for your sin debt. Will you trust Christ as your payment? Will you accept Jesus as your Substitute? Take a few moments and ask Jesus to forgive your sins and trust Him as your Savior.

"Believe on the Lord Jesus Christ, and thou shalt be saved…" (Acts 16:31)

If this copy of *Renewed Strength* was a help to you, and/or if you prayed to receive Christ as your Savior, we'd like to hear from you. Please email us at contact@strengthforlife.church.